KIDS GET CODING

CODING, BUGS, AND FIXES

Heather Lyons & Elizabeth Tweedale

Illustrated by Alex Westgate

Lerner Publications ◆ Minneapolis

Contents

Getting Started

Hi, I'm Data Duck! I'm here to help you learn all about algorithms and bugs. We're going to have lots of fun with activities too!

An algorithm is a simple set of instructions that tells a computer what to do. We're going to learn how to make algorithms, how to try them out, and how to fix them.

DATA DUCK

Here are some key terms you will learn about in this book. Try saying them out loud:

- algorithm
- sequence
- code
- loop
- debug

There are lots of activities in the book for you to try out. There are also some online activities for you to practice with too. For the online activities go to **www.blueshiftcoding.com/kidsgetcoding** and look for the activity with the page number from the book.

Computers Everywhere

Computers are all around us and come in all shapes and sizes. We can use computers to help us do things, such as make phone calls, pay for groceries, and do homework.

Computers are machines, so they aren't very smart on their own. They need instructions to be able to do their tasks. This book will teach you all about how to give computers instructions.

DATA DUCK

A computer's instructions are stored in its memory.

What Can You See?

Can you spot five different types of computers on these pages? What is each one used for?

Turn to page 23 to see the answers.

What Is an Algorithm?

"Algorithm" sounds like a big word, but it just means a series of steps, like those of a recipe.

Computers use algorithms to complete all the tasks we need them to do. We have to give computers clear instructions in the algorithms, so they understand what to do.

5. Brush top and bottom teeth for 2 minutes.

6. Spit out toothpaste.

8. Put toothbrush back in holder.

7. Rinse toothbrush.

DATA DUCK
A computer will use an algorithm to play a movie, search the Internet, or make a phone call.

We use algorithms to do all sorts of everyday jobs. An algorithm for brushing our teeth might look something like this:

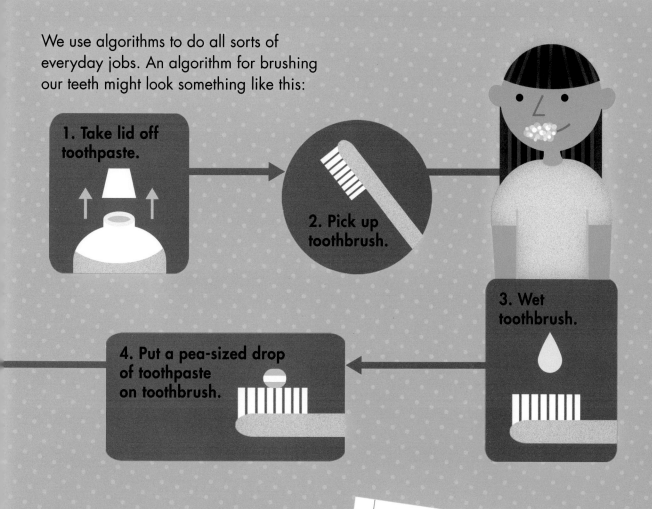

1. Take lid off toothpaste.

2. Pick up toothbrush.

3. Wet toothbrush.

4. Put a pea-sized drop of toothpaste on toothbrush.

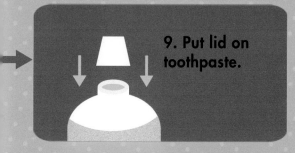

9. Put lid on toothpaste.

Write an Algorithm

Try and write an algorithm for getting ready for school. You'll need to think about all the things you do from the time you wake up, to the time you leave your house.

Turn to page 23 to see an example.

Order, Order!

The steps of an algorithm need to be in the correct order for it to work. The order of steps in an algorithm is called a sequence.

When we write an algorithm, we have to get the sequence of steps right. When we get dressed, for example, it would be silly if we were to put on our shoes before our socks!

DATA DUCK

If the steps of an algorithm are in the wrong order, the algorithm won't work!

Cookie Algorithm

Data duck has written an algorithm to help him make his favorite chocolate chip cookies, but he's got the order of the steps all mixed up. Can you put the steps in the correct order?

Turn to page 23 to see the answers.

Mix together the butter and sugar. Then add in eggs and flour.

OFF

Turn off oven.

Grease baking tray.

Put spoonfuls of mixture onto tray, then bake for 10 minutes.

Eat and enjoy!

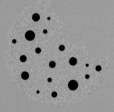

Heat oven to correct temperature.

350F

Make a Move

Algorithms are written in code. This is a kind of language that computers can understand.

When we animate a character on a computer, we use code in the algorithm. It tells the computer where the character should be on the screen.

To make the character move, we need to change the character's position over and over again.

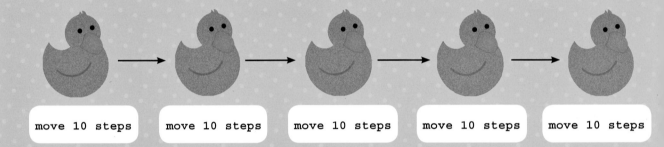

move 10 steps → move 10 steps → move 10 steps → move 10 steps → move 10 steps

DATA DUCK
The things that we can change in the algorithm, such as size, color, and position, are called variables.

If we want to change a character's size, color, or position, we have to change the code.

Spot the Variables

Look closely at the two pictures below. Can you find four different variables in the second picture? Use this list to help you:

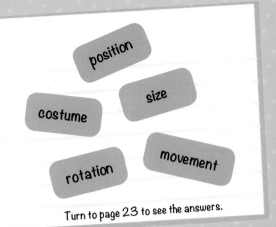

position

costume

size

rotation

movement

Turn to page 23 to see the answers.

For more variable fun, and to try creating an algorithm to make Data Duck move, complete the activity found at: **www.blueshiftcoding.com/kidsgetcoding**

Loop the Loop

Sometimes, we need computers to do a task over and over again. We call these sorts of instructions loops.

We repeat tasks every day. When we walk to school, we repeatedly put one foot in front of the other. When we pedal our bikes, we move our feet round and round. To tell a computer to do these things, we can use loops.

DATA DUCK

We use loops whenever there's an action or instruction we want to repeat. For example, I need a loop to be able to walk all the way across the screen.

On page 10, we had to tell the duck to "move 10 steps" five times to get it to move across the page. Another way to do this is to put one instruction inside a loop, like below:

```
repeat 4 times

move 10 steps
```

Go to **blueshiftcoding.com/kidsgetcoding** for more practice with loops!

{12}

Jam Sandwiches

Imagine you're working in a sandwich shop and need to make the same type of sandwich over and over again. Write instructions to make a jam sandwich. If you had to make ten jam sandwiches, which steps would you put inside your loop?

Turn to page 23 to see an example.

JAM

Predict It

It's helpful if we can predict what an algorithm is meant to do before asking the computer to complete the instruction.

When we press play on a video, for example, we expect a movie to start. But if the steps are in the wrong order, the video won't play!

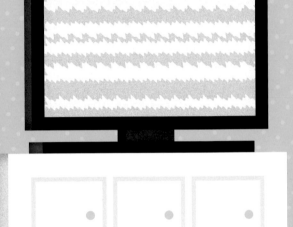

Look at the algorithms below. Can we predict what will happen to Data Duck if we give him the following instructions?

```
change size by one-tenth smaller
```

```
rotate by quarter-turn
```

He's going to become smaller, and twist around by a quarter-turn.

Now, can we predict what will happen if we change the algorithm again?

```
repeat 4 times
    change size by one-tenth smaller

    rotate by quarter-turn
```

He'll make the same movement as the first—but four times! He's going to get smaller four times, and turn four quarter-turns.

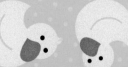

Guess the Shape

Can you predict what shape Data Duck is drawing?

```
Repeat 4 times
    Move 4 steps
      Make a quarter-turn
```

Turn to page 23 to see the answers.

Now, try writing your own instructions to draw:

a cross shape

a T-shape   an L-shape

Can a friend guess the shape by following your instructions?

Decisions, Decisions!

Sometimes, computers need to do something only when a special condition is met. To do this, they use "if statements" to make decisions.

For example, if we tell Data Duck to move to the right, we want to make sure that he doesn't move off the page.

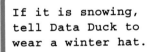

```
repeat 5 times

move 10 steps

If on edge of page, reverse direction
```

The computer needs to make a decision about what Data Duck should wear today. First, it will check the weather. Then, it will look at a series of "if statements" to decide what to do:

```
If it is sunny,
tell Data Duck to
wear sunglasses.
```

```
If it is raining,
tell Data Duck to
bring an umbrella.
```

```
If it is snowing,
tell Data Duck to
wear a winter hat.
```

DATA DUCK

Here's how to make an "if statement":
First, think of a question you'd like to ask
your friend, for example "Is it raining?" If
the answer is "yes," they will have to do
the following: Bring an umbrella.
So the statement is:

```
If it is raining,
bring an umbrella.
```

Make a statement

Let's make an "if statement" game
to play with your friends!
1. Write three different "if statements"
on separate pieces of paper.
2. Put them all into a hat. Shake
them around and then take turns
to be the caller.
3. Each caller reads out an "if
statement" for you and your friends
to follow.

For example, you could use
the following statements:

If you have brown hair,
stand on one foot.

If you are a girl, raise
your hands in the air.

If you are a boy,
touch your toes.

{17}

Search and Sort

Algorithms can also be used to help search for information and sort through it.

For example, a computer can put names in alphabetical order. The computer uses the alphabet to compare letters to see if they come before or after other letters.

DATA DUCK
Algorithms that sort information have two simple parts:
1. Data to be sorted.
2. A rule for sorting the data.

Friend Sorting

Can you sort your friends using a simple rule? Follow these easy steps to search and sort out information about your friends, just like a computer!

1. Write down the names of eight of your friends.

2. Cut up the names and put them in an envelope.

3. Pull out one name at a time and put the names in alphabetical order.

4. Can you think of other ways you might order your friends? For example, would you sort by height or by age?

Catching the Bug

Algorithms are very useful, but sometimes they don't work and we need to find out why. Problems with algorithms are called bugs.

When a programmer reads through an algorithm to find errors and fix them, it is called debugging. Errors might be that a step is missing or that part of the sequence is in the wrong order.

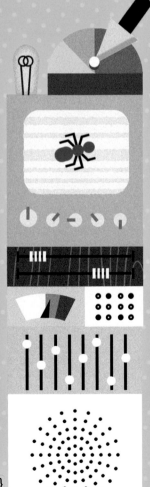

DATA DUCK
When computers were first invented, they were enormous! One day, one of these big computers wouldn't work. When scientists took it apart, they found a moth inside! Some people say this is why we use the word computer "bug."

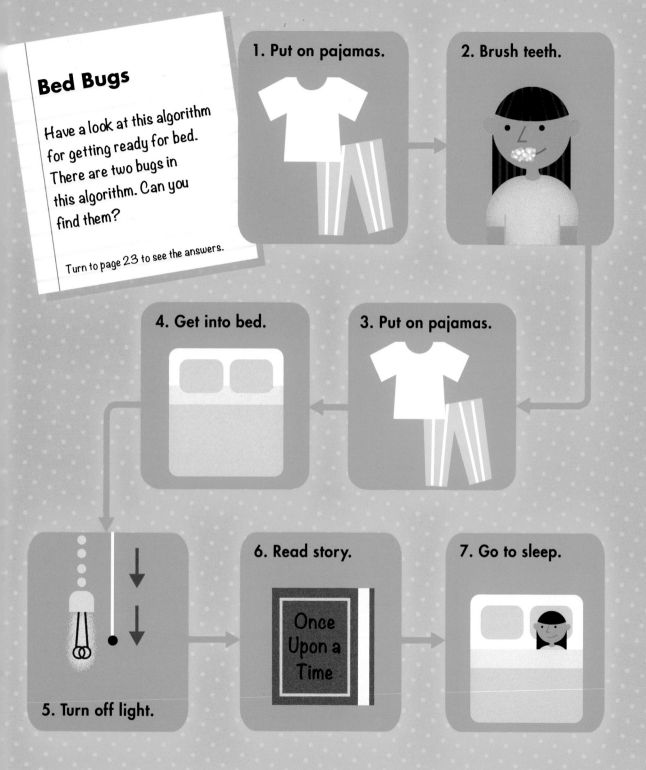

Bed Bugs

Have a look at this algorithm for getting ready for bed. There are two bugs in this algorithm. Can you find them?

Turn to page 23 to see the answers.

1. Put on pajamas.

2. Brush teeth.

4. Get into bed.

3. Put on pajamas.

5. Turn off light.

6. Read story.

7. Go to sleep.

Go to **blueshiftcoding.com/kidsgetcoding** and look at the debugging exercises for more practice.

Extension Activities

Go to **blueshiftcoding.com/kidsgetcoding** for more fun activities and to practice:

- creating algorithms
- using variables
- using loops
- predicting algorithm outcomes
- creating "if statements"
- debugging

Words to Remember

animate: to give the appearance that something on screen has come to life

bug: an error in a computer program

debugging: to find and remove bugs or errors in a computer program

loop: a series of steps with the final step connected to the first step, so the steps are repeated

memory: a way of storing information in a computer

sequence: a particular order in which steps follow one another

variable: something that can be changed or adapted

Activity Answers

Pages 4–5

There are five computers on these pages: TV, phone, tablet, computer, and stereo. Many TVs and stereos have little computer brains that allow them to find and play channels and programs.

Page 7

For example: wake up; get dressed; eat breakfast; brush hair; brush teeth; put on shoes and jacket; pick up backpack

Page 9

1. Heat oven to correct temperature.
2. Mix together the butter and sugar. Then add in eggs and flour.
3. Grease baking tray.
4. Put spoonfuls of mixture onto tray, then bake for 10 minutes.
5. Eat and enjoy.

Page 11

1. Costume: Data Duck is wearing a hat.
2. Position: The mouse and the duck have switched places.
3. Rotation: The mouse is now facing the opposite direction.
4. Size: The mouse is now smaller.

Page 13

You may have a slightly different answer for your jam sandwich making instructions and loop!

1. Put bread loaf on table.
2. Take lid off jam jar.
3. Put jam jar on table.

4. Take two slices of bread and lay out on work surface.
5. Pick up knife.
6. Spread jam on one slice of bread.
7. Put second slice of bread on top of first slice.
8. Cut sandwich in half.

To make ten sandwiches:
1. Put bread loaf on table.
2. Take lid off jam jar.
3. Put jam jar on table.

Then repeat 10 times:
1. Take two slices of bread and lay out on work surface.
2. Pick up knife.
3. Spread jam on one slice of bread.
4. Put second slice of bread on top of first slice.
5. Cut sandwich in half.
6. Put knife down.

Page 15

Data Duck has drawn a square!

Page 21

"Put on pajamas" has been used twice in the algorithm.

"Turn off light" is before "Read story" in the algorithm.

Index

First American edition published in 2017 by Lerner Publishing Group, Inc.

First published in 2016 by Wayland, a division of Hachette Children's Group, an Hachette UK company

Copyright © 2016 by Wayland
Published by arrangement with Wayland

Lerner Publications Company
A division of Lerner Publishing Group, Inc.
241 First Avenue North
Minneapolis, MN 55401 USA

For reading levels and more information, look up this title at www.lernerbooks.com.

Main body text set in Futura Std Book 12/16. Typeface provided by Adobe Systems.

Library of Congress Cataloging-in-Publication Data

Names: Lyons, Heather, 1974- author. | Tweedale, Elizabeth, author. | Westgate, Alex, illustrator.
Title: Coding, bugs, and fixes / written by Heather Lyons and Elizabeth Tweedale ; illustrated by Alex Westgate.
Description: Minneapolis : Lerner Publications, [2017] | Series: Kids get coding | Audience: Ages 6-10. | Audience: K to grade 3. | Includes index.
Identifiers: LCCN 2015044354 (print) | LCCN 2015045675 (ebook) | ISBN 9781512413595 (lb : alk. paper) | ISBN 9781512416008 (pb : alk. paper) | ISBN 9781512413809 (eb pdf)
Subjects: LCSH: Computer programming—Juvenile literature.
Classification: LCC QA76.6 .L885 2017 (print) | LCC QA76.6 (ebook) | DDC 005.1—dc23
LC record available at http://lccn.loc.gov/2015044354

Printed in China 1 – 8/1/16